CYBERSECURITY IN THE AGE OF ESPIONAGE

CYBERSECURITY IN THE AGE OF ESPIONAGE

Protecting Your Digital Life

B. VINCENT

QuantumQuill Press

CONTENTS

Chapter 1: Introduction to Cybersecurity

Figuring out the Significance of Network protection

In the present interconnected world, online protection remains as the key part defending our advanced lives against a variety of dangers. The computerized domain, when a domain of development and opportunity, has turned into a milestone where noxious entertainers, both state-supported and free, compete for control, information, and power. Understanding the significant job network protection plays isn't simply a question of innovative education yet a need for exploring the intricacies of our cutting edge presence.

In this section, we dig into the multi-layered significance of network safety, enlightening its importance across private, corporate, and public areas. We analyze the actual texture of our computerized society, uncovering the weaknesses that hide underneath the surface and the procedures expected to brace our protections. From the inescapable danger of digital secret activities to the tricky strategies of cybercriminals, we defy the unmistakable reality that no edge of the computerized scene stays invulnerable from assault.

In addition, we disentangle the unpredictable snare of interconnectedness that characterizes our advanced presence, wherein the security of people entwines with that of organizations, states, and worldwide organizations. Through enlightening models and certifiable contextual analyses, we explain the significant effect of digital dangers on our day to day routines, highlighting the desperation of supporting our network safety pose.

Eventually, this part fills in as a clarion source of inspiration, encouraging perusers to perceive the basic of network safety not simply as a specialized undertaking but rather as a crucial mainstay of current culture. As we explore the risky waters of the computerized age, it is occupant upon every one of us to embrace the standards of digital flexibility, carefulness, and readiness, for just through aggregate exertion could we at any point desire to defend our advanced future.

Advancement of Digital Assaults

The development of digital assaults is a demonstration of the persistent walk of mechanical advancement and the inventiveness of the individuals who look to take advantage of it. From the beginning long stretches of PC infections to the refined strategies utilized by state-supported entertainers, the scene of digital dangers has gone through a noteworthy change, reshaping the actual texture of our computerized reality.

In this section, we leave on an excursion through time, following the direction of digital assaults from their modest starting points to the current day. We dive into the archives of history, revealing the original minutes and perspective changes that have characterized the advancement of digital fighting and secret activities. From the spearheading exploits of early programmers to the rise of refined cybercrime organizations, every part in this story fills in as a demonstration of the consistently developing nature of the danger scene.

Additionally, we go up against the sobering reality that the weapons contest among assailants and protectors gives no indications of subsiding. As digital dangers fill in complexity and scale, energized by headways in innovation and an undeniably interconnected world, the basic to remain one stride ahead turns into all the really squeezing.

However, in the midst of the consistently present ghost of digital assaults, there exists a hint of something better over the horizon — an acknowledgment that with watchfulness, development, and joint effort, we can construct a future versatile to even the most considerable of enemies. By understanding the past and gaining from its illustrations, we can outline a course toward a safer computerized future, one where the commitment of innovation is acknowledged unafraid of double-dealing or interruption.

At last, this part fills in as a sign of the unique idea of the digital danger scene and the basic to stay watchful despite developing dangers. As we explore the intricacies of the computerized age, furnished with information and assurance, we stand ready to defy the difficulties that lie ahead and manufacture a way toward a more secure, safer tomorrow.

The Advanced Scene

In the immense scope of the computerized scene, a bunch of chances and difficulties anticipates the people who set out to explore its consistently moving landscape. From the multiplication of Web of Things (IoT) gadgets to the omnipresence of distributed computing and virtual entertainment stages, the cutting edge computerized biological system is a dynamic embroidery woven from innumerable interconnected strings.

In this section, we set out on an excursion of investigation, stripping back the layers of intricacy to uncover the hidden elements that shape our computerized lives. We dive into the groundbreaking force of IoT gadgets, inspecting their capability to alter ventures and upgrade accommodation while likewise presenting new security dangers and weaknesses.

Similarly, we examine the outlook changing effect of distributed computing, which has introduced a time of uncommon adaptability and adaptability while testing conventional thoughts of information proprietorship and control. Through wise examination and enlightening models, we uncover the heap manners by which cloud innovations have reshaped the scene of network protection, from the expansion of Programming as a Help (SaaS) answers for the ascent of cross breed and multi-cloud conditions.

Moreover, we stand up to the inescapable impact of virtual entertainment stages, which have become omnipresent installations of present day life, molding the manner in which we convey, associate, and consume data. However, underneath the facade of social network lies a dim underside of protection concerns, information breaks, and deception crusades, highlighting the significance of carefulness and wisdom in the computerized age.

At last, this part fills in as a demonstration of the dynamism and intricacy of the computerized scene, where development and opportunity exist together close by chance and vulnerability. As we explore the complexities of this always developing environment, it is occupant upon us to stay cautious, versatile, and proactive in protecting our advanced characters and resources. Exclusively by understanding the powers at play could we at any point desire to bridle the groundbreaking capability of innovation while alleviating the inborn dangers that go with it.

Key Ideas in Network safety

At the core of the complex universe of online protection lie a progression of key standards and ideas, each filling in as a foundation in the development of strong safeguards against the consistently present danger of digital assaults. In this section, we set out on an excursion of investigation, unwinding the complexities of encryption, confirmation, and chance administration to give perusers a fundamental comprehension of the rules that support compelling network protection rehearses.

As a matter of some importance among these standards is encryption, the bedrock whereupon secure correspondence and information insurance are fabricated. Through the sorcery of cryptographic calculations, encryption changes plaintext into ciphertext, delivering it ambiguous to anybody without the fitting unscrambling key. We investigate the internal operations of encryption calculations, from symmetric and awry encryption to hashing capabilities, revealing insight into the instruments that defend our most delicate data from intrusive eyes.

Similarly crucial for the online protection tool compartment is verification, the interaction by which people and frameworks check their personality and declare their power over computerized assets. Whether through passwords, biometrics, or multifaceted verification, the objective continues as before: to guarantee that main approved elements get sufficiently close to delicate information and assets. By understanding the standards of confirmation, perusers can execute powerful access control systems and upset unapproved access endeavors.

At last, we direct our concentration toward risk the executives, the cycle by which associations distinguish, evaluate, and relieve the heap dangers that hide in the advanced domain. Through a thorough gamble appraisal structure, associations can recognize their most basic resources, assess possible weaknesses, and foster systems to moderate the probability and effect of digital assaults. By embracing a proactive way to deal with risk the executives, associations can limit their openness to digital dangers and construct flexibility notwithstanding difficulty.

Eventually, this part fills in as an introduction on the central ideas that support compelling network protection rehearses. By dominating the standards of encryption, validation, and hazard the board, perusers can leave on an excursion toward more noteworthy security and versatility in an undeniably computerized world. Equipped with information and understanding, we stand ready to defy the difficulties that lie ahead and secure a more brilliant, safer future for a long time into the future.

Chapter 2: Understanding Cyber Threats

Sorts of Computerized Risks

In the enormous and tricky scene of the web, perils slink around each virtual corner, holding on to exploit shortcomings and release ruin on dumbfounded setbacks. In this part, we leave on a careful examination of the different show of advanced perils that plague our modernized world, from the clever risk of malware to the artfulness deception of social planning.

We start by jumping into the shady universe of malware, malicious programming planned to infiltrate, mischief, or take information from laptops and associations. From the malevolent undertakings of contaminations and worms to the cryptic refinement of Trojans and ransomware, we uncover the various designs that malware can take and the staggering results it can deliver upon its setbacks.

Then, we direct our fixation toward the deceptive specialty of phishing, a technique used by cybercriminals to trick individuals into uncovering sensitive information, for instance, passwords, charge card numbers, and individual data. Through astutely made messages, destinations, and messages, phishing attackers exploit human mind science to avoid specific protects and gain unlawful permission to huge assets.

Furthermore, we center around the scourge of ransomware, a particularly poisonous sort of malware that scrambles records or keeps clients out of their systems until a result is paid. We explore the rising of ransomware attacks of late and the tremendous impact they have had on individuals, associations, and, shockingly, essential establishment.

Finally, we dive into the shadowy universe of social planning, wherein attackers control human approach to acting to obtain unapproved induction to systems or information. Through the specialty of impact, confusion, and control, social experts exploit trust, compassion, and interest to evade security controls and enter target associations.

By illuminating the crowd designs and techniques used by advanced risks, this part attempts to arm perusers with the data and care expected to investigate the dangerous waters of the web. By understanding the enemy inside, we might all the more probable protect ourselves against the reliably present dangers that at any point subvert our mechanized lives and livelihoods.

The Occupation of Nation States

In the shadowy area of the web, the lines between battling, observation, and culpability dark as nation states impact electronic progressions to seek after their fundamental objectives and apply impact on the overall stage. In this segment, we dive into the faint universe of state-upheld advanced attacks, examining the motivations, systems, and repercussions of this irrefutably undeniable sort of computerized risk.

At the center of state-upheld computerized attacks lies the fundamental essential to secure a high ground in the worldwide field, whether by taking sensitive information, disturbing essential structure, or applying influence over new governing bodies and peoples. From the mysterious entrance of government associations to the improper mischief of energy cross sections and money related systems, state-upheld computerized attacks address a strong weapon in the munititions store of present day battling and reconnaissance.

What's more, we face the sobering reality that the location of advanced battle is stacked with ambiguity and weakness, where attribution is ordinarily tricky and the rules of responsibility stay overcast, most ideal situation. In a period where computerized limits offer a negligible cost, high-impact strategy for applying power and effect, country states continuously view the web as a milestone where wars are sought after in the shadows, far from as per everybody and the goals of customary battling.

Nonetheless, amidst the creating phantom of computerized battling and covert work, there exists a hint of something better over the horizon — an affirmation that with support, joint exertion, and prudence, we can manufacture a future where the norms and rules of the web are addressed by guidelines of straightforwardness, obligation, and normal respect. By developing worldwide associations and trade, we can participate to confront the normal challenges introduced by state-upheld computerized risks and layout a course toward a more secure and stable mechanized future.

At last, this part fills in as a sobering indication of the confounding trade between development, legislative issues, and security in the mechanized age. By understanding the motivations and techniques of nation states in the web, we can all the more promptly positioned ourselves to investigate the global minefield and safeguard our electronic power in an unquestionably unsteady and problematic world.

Insider Risks

In the area of organization security, the best perils habitually come from within, as accepted individuals with limited permission to fragile systems and information sell out that trust for individual expansion or horrible purposes. In this segment, we center around the tricky risk introduced by insider attacks, examining the motivations, methods, and consequences of these subtle shows of deceiving.

Insider perils come in many designs, going from disappointed agents searching for retribution to unplanned partners constrained by outside adversaries. Whether through intentional harm, theft of safeguarded development, or unintentional recklessness, insiders might conceivably bring about basic naughtiness for affiliations, much of the time with far reaching results.

Furthermore, we oppose the off-kilter truth that insider perils are not just a speculative concern yet rather an unforgiving reality looked by relationship of all sizes and undertakings. From high-profile data breaks to corporate mystery exercises shocks, the titles are spilling over with examples of insiders misusing their entry and deluding the trust put in them by their supervisors.

Nonetheless, amidst the creating risk of insider risks, there exists a hint of something to look forward to — an affirmation that with genuine controls, noticing, and planning, affiliations can ease the perils introduced by insider attacks and shield their most critical assets. By executing solid access controls, coordinating standard surveys, and developing a culture of wellbeing care, affiliations can diminish the likelihood of insider events and recognize them before they develop into endlessly out crises.

Finally, this part fills in as a suggestion to affiliations everywhere, uplifting them to see the risk introduced by insiders and track down proactive ways of shielding against it. By understanding the motivations and strategies for insider attackers, affiliations can all the more probable safeguard themselves from unfairness and safeguard their most significant assets in an unquestionably unpleasant high level scene.

Emerging Risks

As advancement continues to foster hazardously quick, so too do the perils that conceal in the mechanized shadows, constantly changing and progressing to exploit new shortcomings and departure provisions. In this part, we peer into the valuable stone piece of organization security, extending our look toward the horizon to reveal the emerging risks that loom not excessively far off, doing whatever it takes to disturb the delicate equilibrium of our high level world.

One such emerging peril is the rising of PC based insight controlled computerized attacks, where artificial intelligence estimations are weaponized to robotize and redesign the limits of threatening performers. From man-put forth insight driven phishing attempts to not well arranged attacks on computer based intelligence structures, these emerging perils address a great test to traditional safety officers, requiring new techniques and procedures to recognize and ease.

Moreover, we challenge the creating apparition of deepfakes, hypersensible controls of sound, video, and imagery that are muddled from this present reality. As deepfake development ends up being logically complicated and open, the potential for threatening performers to weaponize it for proclamation, disinformation, and blackmail addresses a colossal risk to individuals, affiliations, and society at large.

Likewise, we peer into the quantum future, where the presence of quantum figuring promises to change cryptography and render an impressive parcel of our continuous security shows obsolete. While the normal benefits of quantum figuring are gigantic, so too are the risks, as quantum-engaged attacks do whatever it may take to undermine the underpinnings of our mechanized structure and upset the delicate generally speaking impact in the web.

Notwithstanding, amidst the oncoming phantom of emerging risks, there exists a commitment of something better — an affirmation that with hunch, improvement, and facilitated exertion, we can change and create to address the troubles that lie ahead. By investing assets into imaginative energy, developing interdisciplinary joint exertion, and propelling a culture of organization security care, we can stay one step ready and safeguard our modernized future from here onward, indefinitely.

In the end, this segment fills in as a wellspring of motivation, empowering accomplices across the electronic climate to see the distress of addressing emerging risks and track down proactive ways of safeguarding against them. By embracing improvement, embracing joint exertion, and embracing adaptability, we can adjust to the circumstance and develop a future where the responsibility of development is recognized unafraid of misleading or interference.

Chapter 3: Securing Your Digital Life

Individual Digital Cleanliness

In the huge and steadily growing computerized scene, people stand as the primary line of protection against a horde of digital dangers that hide in the shadows, holding on to take advantage of weaknesses and unleash ruin on clueless casualties. In this part, we dive into the domain of individual digital cleanliness, furnishing perusers with the information and devices expected to sustain their advanced protections and shield their web-based characters.

At the center of individual digital cleanliness lies the acknowledgment that fundamental security practices can go quite far in moderating the gamble of succumbing to digital assaults. We start by stressing the significance of involving solid and remarkable passwords for each internet based account, as well as the need of consistently refreshing passwords to defeat possible breaks. Moreover, we dive into the significance of empowering two-factor verification (2FA) at every possible opportunity, adding an additional layer of safety to delicate records and exchanges.

Besides, we investigate the basic job of programming updates and fixes in keeping up with the security of gadgets and applications. By guaranteeing that working frameworks, antivirus programming, and different projects are state-of-the-art, people can fix known weaknesses and decrease the gamble of abuse by cybercriminals. We likewise give direction on designing security settings and authorizations for applications and administrations, enabling perusers to assume command over their advanced impression and limit openness to nosy information assortment rehearses.

Besides, we dive into the significance of pursuing safe perusing routines, including practicing alert while tapping on joins or downloading documents from obscure sources. Using secure internet browsers, promotion blockers, and virtual confidential organizations (VPNs), people can relieve the gamble of experiencing malware, phishing tricks, and other web-based dangers.

Eventually, this part fills in as a guide for people trying to improve their network safety pose and safeguard their computerized lives in an undeniably threatening web-based climate. By embracing the standards of individual digital cleanliness and taking on proactive security rehearses, perusers can diminish their helplessness to digital dangers and explore the advanced scene with certainty and versatility.

Getting Gadgets and Organizations

In the interconnected snare of our computerized lives, the security of our gadgets and organizations shapes the establishment whereupon our web-based wellbeing rests. In this section, we leave on an excursion through the complexities of getting the horde gadgets that populate our homes, work environments, and pockets, as well as the organizations that interface them to the huge territory of the web.

We start by investigating the scene of gadget security, offering pragmatic direction on protecting PCs, cell phones, and Web of Things (IoT) gadgets against digital dangers. From empowering gadget encryption and biometric validation to introducing trustworthy antivirus programming and firewalls, we engage perusers to find proactive ways to invigorate the security of their computerized endpoints.

Additionally, we dive into the domain of organization security, analyzing the different dangers that sneak inside the advanced ether and the procedures expected to alleviate them. Whether getting a home Wi-Fi network against unapproved access or executing hearty edge guards in a professional workplace, we give experiences into the devices and methods that can assist with defending organizations against digital interruptions and information breaks.

Moreover, we investigate the developing significance of getting remote access and virtual confidential organizations (VPNs) in a time where remote work and working from home have turned into the standard. By scrambling information transmissions and getting distant endpoints, people and associations can alleviate the gamble of capture and unapproved access by digital enemies.

At last, this part fills in as a signal of direction for people and associations looking to strengthen their computerized foundation against the consistently present danger of digital assaults. By embracing the standards of gadget and organization security and taking on proactive measures to safeguard against weaknesses and exploits, perusers can explore the advanced scene with certainty and versatility, it are free from even a hint of harm to know that their computerized resources.

Security and Information Assurance

During a time where individual information has turned into an item exchanged on the computerized commercial center, shielding one's security and safeguarding delicate data has never been more basic. In this part, we dive into the complexities of security and information assurance, outfitting perusers with the information and apparatuses expected to explore the intricacies of the computerized biological system while shielding their most valuable resource — their own data.

We start by investigating the principal significance of protection in the computerized age, looking at the ramifications of omnipresent information assortment and the disintegration of individual security in a period of unavoidable observation. From the following of online way of behaving by publicists to the mass assortment of metadata by government organizations, we shed light on the bunch manners by which people's security is compromised in the computerized domain.

Besides, we dig into the legitimate and administrative scene encompassing security and information insurance, offering direction on exploring the maze of protection regulations and guidelines that administer the assortment, use, and capacity of individual information. From the European Association's Overall Information Assurance Guideline (GDPR) to the California Purchaser Security Act (CCPA), we give bits of knowledge into the limitations of people and associations in defending security privileges and safeguarding individual information.

Moreover, we investigate functional methodologies for protecting individual data and improving security in daily existence. From limiting information openness via virtual entertainment stages to utilizing encryption devices and secure correspondence channels, we engage perusers to assume command over their computerized impression and cutoff the gamble of unapproved access and abuse of their own information.

At last, this part fills in as a revitalizing sob for people to recover their security in an undeniably interconnected world. By embracing the standards of security and information assurance and upholding for more noteworthy straightforwardness and responsibility in the computerized environment, perusers can affirm their freedoms and shield their own data from according to digital enemies and information expedites the same.

Network safety Mindfulness

In the fight against digital dangers, information is the most remarkable weapon available to us. In this part, we enlighten the significance of network protection mindfulness and schooling, engaging people and associations to become proactive safeguards of their computerized domains.

We start by investigating the inescapable absence of network safety mindfulness that plagues society, featuring the stunning predominance of digital assaults that come from human blunder and carelessness. From succumbing to phishing tricks to coincidentally tapping on noxious connections, we uncover the horde manners by which people's absence of mindfulness adds to the outcome of digital enemies.

Besides, we dig into the basic job of schooling and preparing in developing a culture of online protection mindfulness inside associations. By furnishing workers with the information and abilities expected to distinguish and answer digital dangers, associations can relieve the gamble of information breaks and digital assaults coming from insider dangers and human blunder.

Moreover, we investigate the significance of cultivating network safety mindfulness among the overall population, engaging people to safeguard themselves against digital dangers and settle on informed conclusions about their internet based conduct. Through open mindfulness crusades, instructive drives, and local area outreach endeavors, we can raise the shared mindset about the significance of network protection and motivate people to find proactive ways to shield their advanced lives.

At last, this section fills in as a source of inspiration for people and associations to focus on network safety mindfulness and training as a foundation of their online protection methodology. By cultivating a culture of mindfulness, cautiousness, and obligation, we can reverse the situation against digital dangers and construct a more secure, safer computerized future for all.

Chapter 4: Cybersecurity in the Workplace

Corporate Digital Dangers

In the merciless universe of business, the stakes of online protection are higher than at any other time. In this section, we dive into the one of a kind online protection challenges that organizations face, exploring the tricky waters of information breaks, licensed innovation robbery, and store network weaknesses that take steps to sabotage the actual texture of hierarchical security.

At the very front of corporate digital dangers lies the apparition of information breaks, wherein delicate data like client information, monetary records, and exclusive insider facts fall into some unacceptable hands. We investigate the heap manners by which information breaks can happen, from malignant hacking endeavors to coincidental worker mistakes, and the significant outcomes they can have on the impacted association, including monetary misfortunes, reputational harm, and legitimate liabilities.

Besides, we focus on the treacherous danger of protected innovation robbery, wherein contenders, cybercriminals, and country states look to take important proprietary advantages, licenses, and innovative work information. Through designated digital assaults and undercover work strategies, foes can acquire an upper hand to the detriment of development, imagination, and financial flourishing.

Moreover, we look at the weaknesses innate in worldwide stock chains, where interconnected organizations of providers, merchants, and accomplices make a snare of conditions that can be taken advantage of by digital enemies. From outsider information breaks to production network assaults focusing on basic foundation and assembling processes, we uncover the secret dangers that hide underneath the outer layer of worldwide business and exchange.

At last, this section fills in as a reminder for organizations all over the place, encouraging them to perceive the earnestness of addressing corporate digital dangers and find proactive ways to safeguard against them. By embracing a comprehensive way to deal with online protection that envelops individuals, cycles, and innovation, associations can relieve the gamble of digital dangers and fabricate versatility despite misfortune, guaranteeing their endurance and outcome in an undeniably computerized world.

Building an Online protection Technique

In the consistently developing scene of digital dangers, associations should arm themselves with an extensive online protection technique to explore the fierce waters of the computerized domain. In this section, we set out on an excursion through the complexities of network safety technique improvement, giving associations the direction and devices expected to reinforce their guards and moderate the gamble of digital assaults.

At the core of any successful online protection procedure lies a careful comprehension of the association's gamble scene and network safety act. We start by illustrating the significance of leading an exhaustive gamble evaluation, recognizing expected dangers, weaknesses, and resources in danger. By surveying the probability and possible effect of different digital dangers, associations can focus on their network protection endeavors and dispense assets actually to address the most squeezing chances.

Besides, we dive into the basic parts of a vigorous network protection procedure, including occurrence reaction arranging, worker preparing, and innovation execution. Through the improvement of occurrence reaction plans and playbooks, associations can plan for and relieve the effect of digital episodes, limiting margin time, monetary misfortunes, and reputational harm in case of a break.

Moreover, we investigate the significance of representative preparation and mindfulness in encouraging a culture of network safety inside the association. By furnishing representatives with the information and abilities expected to perceive and answer digital dangers, associations can engage their labor force to become dynamic members in the safeguard against digital assaults, as opposed to accidental accessories.

At last, this section fills in as an outline for associations looking to create and carry out an extensive network protection methodology. By embracing a proactive way to deal with online protection that envelops risk the board, episode reaction, and representative preparation, associations can strengthen their guards and relieve the gamble of digital assaults, guaranteeing their proceeded with progress and versatility in an undeniably computerized world.

Getting Remote Work

Right after worldwide changes in work elements, remote work has become more predominant than any other time, introducing the two open doors and difficulties for associations endeavoring to keep up with network protection versatility. In this section, we explore the intricacies of getting remote work game plans, offering bits of knowledge and best practices to moderate the security chances related with dispersed labor forces.

Remote work presents a heap of safety suggestions, as representatives access corporate organizations and delicate information from outside the conventional limits of the workplace. We start by inspecting the novel difficulties presented by remote access, including the expanded gamble of unapproved access, information breaks, and insider dangers. By understanding the security ramifications of remote work, associations can go to proactive lengths to get remote passages, for example, carrying out multifaceted confirmation, virtual confidential organizations (VPNs), and strong endpoint security arrangements.

Additionally, we dig into the significance of getting far off endpoints, like workstations, cell phones, and tablets, which act as the essential passages for telecommuters. By executing endpoint safety efforts like gadget encryption, secure design the board, and remote wipe abilities, associations can limit the gamble of unapproved access and information misfortune from compromised gadgets.

Moreover, we investigate the security ramifications of distant correspondence and cooperation instruments, for example, video conferencing stages and cloud-based efficiency suites. By encoding correspondences, upholding access controls, and observing for dubious movement, associations can guarantee the privacy, respectability, and accessibility of delicate data divided between telecommuters.

Eventually, this part fills in as a guide for associations looking to get their remote workplaces and enable their dispersed labor force to work securely and safely from anyplace. By embracing a comprehensive way to deal with remote work security that envelops remote access, endpoint security, and specialized devices, associations can moderate the gamble of digital dangers and empower their labor force to stay useful and versatile in an undeniably distant world.

Joint effort and Organizations

In the steadily developing scene of digital dangers, associations can't bear to go solo. In this section, we investigate the significance of joint effort and associations in upgrading aggregate network protection strength and guarding against the horde dangers that prowl in the advanced domain.

At the core of powerful network safety joint effort lies the acknowledgment that no association exists in separation, and digital dangers rise above geological and sectoral limits. We start by analyzing the job of public-private organizations in encouraging data sharing, danger knowledge trade, and joint reaction endeavors between government organizations, industry partners, and online protection sellers. By utilizing the aggregate mastery and assets of assorted partners, associations can acquire significant bits of knowledge into arising dangers and upgrade their capacity to distinguish, forestall, and answer digital assaults.

In addition, we dive into the significance of cooperation inside the confidential area, as associations share best practices, examples learned, and danger knowledge to reinforce their aggregate safeguards against digital dangers. Through industry-explicit Data Sharing and Investigation Focuses (ISACs), area explicit online protection unions, and cross-industry cooperation drives, associations can profit from the aggregate insight and experience of their companions and fortify their versatility to digital assaults.

Moreover, we investigate the job of worldwide coordinated effort in tending to worldwide digital dangers, as countries cooperate to lay out standards, principles, and conventions for dependable conduct in the internet. By encouraging political discourse, advancing online protection limit constructing, and working with cross-line participation, countries can upgrade their capacity to forestall and relieve digital assaults and advance soundness and security in the computerized domain.

Eventually, this section fills in as a source of inspiration for associations, legislatures, and partners across the computerized biological system to embrace cooperation and organization as fundamental mainstays of compelling network safety. By cooperating to share data, pool assets, and direction reaction endeavors, we can construct a more grounded, stronger digital protection environment and shield our aggregate computerized future for a long time into the future.

Chapter 5: The Future of Cybersecurity

Arising Advances and Patterns

As we stand on the slope of another period characterized by quick mechanical headway, the scene of network safety is ready for significant change. In this part, we set out on an excursion through the wilderness of arising innovations and patterns, investigating the state of the art developments and developing dangers that will shape the fate of network protection.

At the bleeding edge of this mechanical unrest lie a bunch of pivotal developments, from man-made reasoning and AI to quantum figuring and blockchain. We dig into the likely uses of these advancements in network safety, from simulated intelligence controlled danger discovery and reaction to quantum-safe encryption and decentralized confirmation components. By tackling the force of these arising advancements, associations can improve their capacity to identify, forestall, and answer digital dangers continuously, introducing another period of proactive and versatile network safety protections.

Additionally, we stand up to the sobering reality that with development comes risk, as cybercriminals influence similar advancements to send off progressively complex and designated assaults. We investigate arising patterns in digital dangers, for example, simulated intelligence controlled assaults that influence AI calculations to sidestep conventional security guards, ransomware-as-a-administration plots that commoditize cybercrime, and production network goes after that target confided in sellers and accomplices. By understanding these arising dangers, associations can all the more likely set themselves up to safeguard against developing assault strategies and remain one stride in front of digital enemies.

At last, this part fills in as a signal of direction for associations looking to explore the dubious territory representing things to come of network safety. By embracing arising innovations, remaining watchful to arising dangers, and taking on a proactive and versatile way to deal with network protection, associations can situate themselves for outcome in an undeniably mind boggling and interconnected computerized scene.

Network safety Guidelines and Arrangements

In the quickly developing scene of network safety, the administrative climate assumes an essential part in molding the ways of behaving and practices of associations and people the same. In this part, we dive into the complicated trap of network protection guidelines and approaches, investigating their suggestions for organizations, legislatures, and society at large.

We start by looking at the steadily growing administrative scene encompassing network safety, which envelops an interwoven of regulations, guidelines, and industry principles intended to safeguard delicate information and defend basic framework. From the European Association's Overall Information Insurance Guideline (GDPR) to industry-explicit systems, for example, the Installment Card Industry Information Security Standard (PCI DSS), associations should explore a complicated snare of consistence prerequisites to guarantee the security and protection of their computerized resources.

Also, we investigate the ramifications of administrative consistence for associations, including the expenses and difficulties related with carrying out and keeping up with network safety controls, as well as the expected results of resistance, like fines, punishments, and reputational harm. By understanding the administrative scene and its suggestions, associations can foster strong consistence projects and administration designs to relieve risk and guarantee adherence to relevant regulations and guidelines.

Besides, we look at the job of government offices and worldwide associations in authorizing network protection guidelines and arrangements, as well as the difficulties they face in staying up with quickly developing digital dangers. From policing entrusted with exploring cybercrime to administrative bodies liable for drafting and upholding network protection guidelines, states assume a significant part in molding the network protection scene and advancing responsibility and straightforwardness in the computerized domain.

Eventually, this part fills in as a source of inspiration for associations to focus on network safety consistence and administration as fundamental parts of their gamble the executives systems. By embracing a proactive way to deal with administrative consistence, associations can fabricate entrust with clients, accomplices, and partners, show their obligation to safeguarding delicate information, and explore the intricacies of the administrative scene with certainty and flexibility.

Moral and Social Ramifications

In the computerized age, where our lives are progressively entwined with innovation, the moral and social ramifications of network protection pose a potential threat not too far off. In this section, we set out on an excursion to investigate the multi-layered moral and social contemplations that support the field of network safety, looking at the complicated exchange between innovation, security, and common liberties.

We start by thinking about the significant effect of network safety on individual security and computerized freedoms, as the tireless walk of mechanical advancement takes steps to dissolve the limits among public and confidential circles. From omnipresent observation and information assortment to the disintegration of namelessness and free articulation on the web, we face the difficulties presented by the commodification of individual information and the disintegration of security in the advanced age.

In addition, we dig into the moral predicaments innate in network protection exploration, improvement, and practice, as technologists wrestle with inquiries of obligation, responsibility, and potentially negative results. From the moral ramifications of creating hostile digital weapons to the moral contemplations of weakness revelation and dependable divulgence strategies, we investigate the ethical intricacies that emerge when innovation meets with human way of behaving and cultural standards.

Besides, we inspect the more extensive cultural ramifications of network safety, remembering its effect for monetary flourishing, public safety, and popularity based administration. From the weakening impacts of digital assaults on basic foundation to the disintegration of public confidence in just establishments directly following political race impedance and disinformation crusades, we defy the broad results of digital dangers on the structure holding the system together.

Eventually, this section fills in as a source of inspiration for people, associations, and policymakers to wrestle with the moral and social ramifications of network protection and endeavor to work out some kind of harmony among security and security, development and obligation. By embracing moral standards like straightforwardness, responsibility, and regard for common freedoms, we can construct a more comprehensive, impartial, and secure computerized future for all.

The Way ahead

As we peer into the fate of network safety, the street ahead is laden with the two difficulties and potential open doors. In this last section, we consider the illustrations took in, the headway made, and the excursion that lies ahead as we endeavor to fabricate a safer and versatile computerized world.

We start by recognizing the consistently advancing nature of digital dangers and the requirement for nonstop variation and development in our way to deal with network protection. From the quick multiplication of new assault vectors to the development of novel advances and patterns, the scene of online protection is in a steady condition of transition, requiring carefulness, spryness, and premonition from all partners.

Additionally, we investigate the difficulties presented by the augmenting network safety abilities hole, as associations battle to select and hold qualified online protection experts despite remarkable interest. By putting resources into instruction, preparing, and labor force improvement drives, we can develop the up and coming age of network protection ability and outfit them with the abilities and information expected to safeguard against arising dangers.

Besides, we analyze the job of cooperation and association in reinforcing our aggregate network safety strength, as associations, legislatures, and partners cooperate to share data, pool assets, and direction reaction endeavors. By cultivating a culture of coordinated effort, trust, and straightforwardness, we can fabricate a more grounded, stronger digital safeguard biological system fit for enduring even the most modern digital assaults.

Eventually, this part fills in as an energizing sob for activity, encouraging partners across the computerized environment to embrace the difficulties and valuable open doors that lie ahead and cooperate to fabricate a safer and versatile computerized future. By embracing development, cooperation, and mindful direct, we can conquer the difficulties of network protection and make an existence where innovation fills in as a power for good, as opposed to a wellspring of dread and vulnerability.

Conclusion

Recap of Key Bits of knowledge

As we come to the finish of our investigation into network safety, it's fundamental to return to the essential bits of knowledge and revelations uncovered all through our excursion. In this part, we ponder the critical important points from every section, refining the abundance of data into noteworthy experiences that perusers can convey forward as they continued looking for a safer computerized future.

All through the book, we've dove into different parts of network safety, from understanding the advancing danger scene to executing strong safety efforts in both individual and expert spaces. We've investigated the complexities of digital dangers, going from refined country state assaults to the deceptive dangers presented by insider dangers and arising advancements. En route, we've analyzed the basic job of cooperation, schooling, and moral contemplations in forming the eventual fate of network protection.

By recapping the critical experiences from every part, we support the basic information expected to successfully explore the intricacies of network safety. From the significance of solid passwords and customary programming updates to the requirement for proactive episode reaction arranging and worldwide collaboration, every knowledge fills in as a structure block in developing an exhaustive network safety technique.

Eventually, this recap fills in as a sign of the multi-layered nature of network protection and the continuous endeavors expected to remain in front of developing dangers. By assimilating these critical bits of knowledge and applying them by and by, perusers can reinforce their guards, moderate gamble, and add to the aggregate work to construct a more secure and stronger computerized world.

Source of inspiration

As we close our investigation of network safety, it's essential to perceive that information alone isn't sufficient to protect against the horde dangers hiding in the advanced scene. In this segment, we issue a source of inspiration, encouraging perusers to decipher the bits of knowledge acquired from this book into substantial moves toward improve their online protection act and add to a more secure computerized climate.

The most important phase in noting this source of inspiration is mindfulness. By bringing issues to light of the always present risks of digital dangers and the significance of network safety best practices, people and associations can enable themselves to proactively perceive and answer possible dangers. From remaining watchful against phishing tricks to rehearsing great digital cleanliness, each individual plays a part to play in guarding against digital assaults.

In addition, schooling and preparing are fundamental parts of any powerful network safety methodology. By putting resources into continuous schooling and preparing programs, associations can guarantee that their labor force stays exceptional on the most recent dangers, patterns, and best practices in network protection. From fundamental security mindfulness preparing for representatives to particular specialized preparing for network protection experts, persistent learning is vital to remaining on the ball in a steadily changing danger scene.

Moreover, cooperation is basic in the battle against digital dangers. By encouraging associations with industry peers, government organizations, and online protection merchants, associations can share danger insight, pool assets, and direction reaction endeavors to moderate the effect of digital assaults. Together, we can construct a more grounded, stronger digital guard environment equipped for enduring even the most complex dangers.

Eventually, this source of inspiration is an update that network safety is a common obligation that requires aggregate exertion and responsibility from all partners. By finding a way proactive ways to upgrade network safety mindfulness, training, and coordinated effort, we can reinforce our safeguards, relieve hazard, and construct a more secure and safer computerized future for a long time into the future.

Vision for What's to come

As we plan ahead for network safety, it's crucial for cast our look into the great beyond and imagine the sort of computerized world we seek to make. In this segment, we frame a dream for a safer and strong future, driven by development, joint effort, and mindful lead.

At the core of this vision lies the acknowledgment that innovation will keep on developing at a quick speed, introducing the two potential open doors and difficulties for network safety. From the inescapable reception of arising advances, for example, man-made reasoning and quantum registering to the expansion of Web of Things (IoT) gadgets and brilliant framework, the computerized scene of tomorrow will be incomprehensibly not quite the same as the one we know today.

In this future, online protection will be coordinated into the texture of our computerized society, with security and protection by plan standards implanted into the advancement lifecycle of innovation items and administrations. By focusing on security all along and embracing a proactive and versatile way to deal with network safety, associations can incorporate strength into their frameworks and foundation, guaranteeing they can endure even the most complex digital assaults.

Also, cooperation will be the foundation of our aggregate network protection endeavors, as associations, state run administrations, and partners cooperate to share danger knowledge, pool assets, and direction reaction endeavors. By cultivating a culture of joint effort, trust, and straightforwardness, we can fabricate a more grounded, stronger digital safeguard environment equipped for recognizing, forestalling, and relieving digital dangers progressively.

Moreover, moral contemplations will direct our activities in the computerized domain, guaranteeing that innovation is created and sent in a way that regards common liberties, protection, and cultural qualities. By embracing morals and capable lead in network protection examination, improvement, and practice, we can fabricate entrust with clients, encourage development, and advance the mindful utilization of innovation to assist society.

At last, this vision for the fate of network safety is one of trust and hopefulness, grounded in the conviction that by cooperating and embracing development, coordinated effort, and morals, we can defeat the difficulties of online protection and make an existence where innovation fills in as a power for good, as opposed to a wellspring of dread and vulnerability.

Last Contemplations

As we draw our excursion through the domain of network safety to a nearby, considering the significant meaning of this field in forming the fate of our computerized world is fundamental. In this last segment, we offer a few shutting reflections on the significance of network safety and offer our thanks to perusers for their commitment and obligation to this basic undertaking.

All through this book, we've investigated the intricacies of network protection, from understanding the developing danger scene to executing vigorous safety efforts and encouraging a culture of cooperation and moral direct. We've stood up to the sobering truth of digital dangers and the consistently present risks they posture to people, associations, and society at large. However, in the midst of the difficulties, we've likewise witnessed the vast capability of network safety to enable us, safeguard us, and prepare for a more splendid computerized future.

As we ponder the illustrations gained and the experiences acquired from our investigation, obviously the excursion towards a safer and versatile computerized world is continuous and requires the aggregate exertion, everything being equal. It requires carefulness, training, coordinated effort, and a relentless obligation to moral lead and dependable utilization of innovation. It expects us to stay cautious against arising dangers, to consistently adjust and enhance in our way to deal with network safety, and to encourage a culture of safety and flexibility in all that we do.

All things being equal, we stretch out our genuine appreciation to perusers for going along with us on this excursion and for their immovable devotion to the reason for network safety. Whether you're a singular trying to safeguard your computerized character or an association endeavoring to protect your delicate information, your obligation to network safety is fundamental in building a more secure and safer advanced world for all. Together, let us keep on taking a stab at greatness, to push the limits of development, and to maintain the genuinely honorable upsides, trust, and obligation in all that we do.

Much thanks to you for your enthusiasm, your devotion, and your unfaltering obligation to the fundamental mission of online protection. Together, we can beat the difficulties ahead and fabricate a more brilliant, safer future for a long time into the future.